Edition Schott

Kamran Ince

b. 1960

MKG Variations

for Guitar
für Gitarre

Edited by/Herausgegeben von
Lily Afshar

ED 30020
ISMN M-60001-057-8

www.schott-music.com

Mainz · London · Madrid · New York · Paris · Prague · Tokyo · Toronto
© 2009 SCHOTT MUSIC CORPORATION · Printed in USA

Preface

MKG Variations for solo guitar was commissioned by Marlene Guzman and originally written for solo cello in February-March 1999. The version for guitar was created in the summer of 2001.

Guitarist Lily Afshar's help in creating the version for guitar was invaluable. The original version of the work took advantage of the sonorous qualities of the open strings on the cello; to create the same effect on guitar, the entire piece was transposed up a whole tone. Many of the chords and harmonics did not speak the same way on guitar, so they were re-voiced. Increasing the piece's tempi made the work more appropriate for guitar, as well. This version shares the same essence as the earlier cello arrangement, though it is made organic for guitar. I liken this process to something which happens regularly in theater: two actors playing exactly the same role.

The piece stems from a spiritual impulse. The first idea—a calm yet anticipatory stasis—acts as a theme which is then explored in a series of variations. These range from a passionate expression of the theme to a percussive one; from an angry one to an extremely delicate one; from one reminiscent of Bach to one that is both fleeting and frozen in time; and to one that is more raw and unforgiving. The work closes with a final presentation of the original theme that dissolves into silence, its origin.

Kamran Ince
2009

This work is recorded by Lily Afshar on her CD, *Possession*. Archer Records (ARCC1919).

MKG Variations
for guitar

Arranged by Lily Afshar and Kamran Ince
Editing and fingering by Lily Afshar

Kamran Ince
(2001)

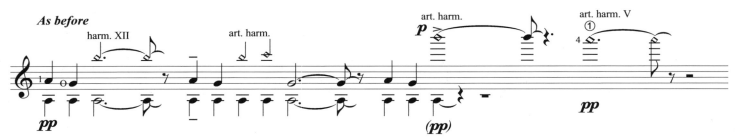

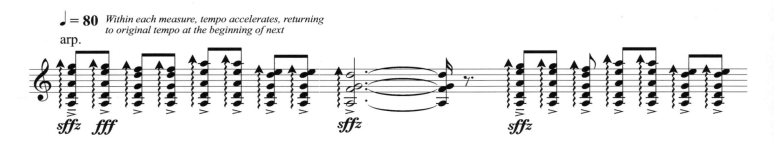

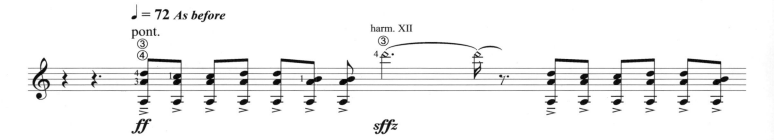

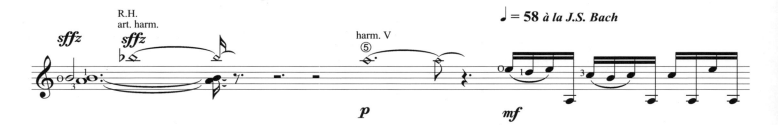

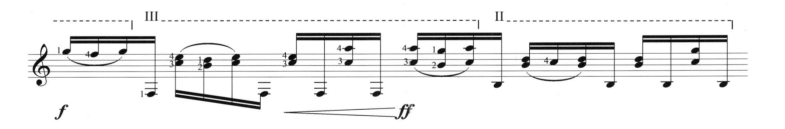

4

♩ = 52 *Generally, as the line ascends, tempo should increase,*
as it descends, tempo should decrease

Each note should sound individually with slow strokes

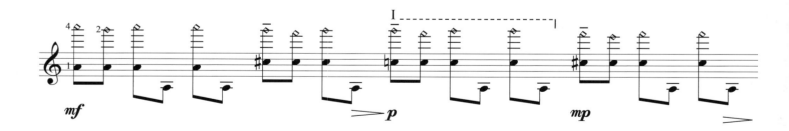

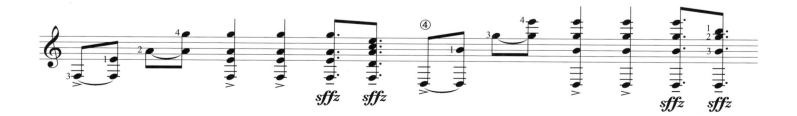

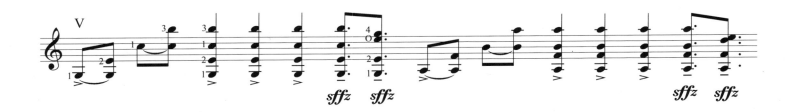

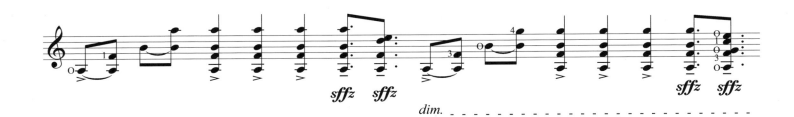

8

III   II _

_ ⌐   V

art. harm.

♩ = 63 *Tempo primo, and whimsically uneven*

R.H. _